MEGA TRUCKS

BARRON'S

First edition for the United States and Canada published in 2016
by Barron's Educational Series, Inc.
Copyright © 2005, 2014 by Picthall and Gunzi,
An imprint of Award Publications Limited, The Old Riding School,
The Welbeck Estate, Worksop, S80 3LR

Written and edited by: Deborah Murrell and Christiane Gunzi
Designer: Paul Calver
Design assistance: Ray Bryant & Gill Shaw
Commercial vehicle consultant: Peter J. Davies
Education consultants: Diana Bentley, MA Advanced Diploma in Children's Literature;
Jane Whitwell, Diploma in Special Education Needs

All inquiries should be addressed to:
Barron's Educational Series, Inc.
250 Wireless Boulevard, Hauppauge, New York 11788
www.barronseduc.com

Thank you to the following companies and individuals for the use of their images:
Caterpillar; Daimler Chrysler Ltd; Ford Motor Company; Freightliner Group; Leibherr
(manufacturer of the world's largest range of mobile cranes); McNeilus; Oshkosh Truck
Corporation, Oshkosh, Wisconsin USA; Scania Image Desk

BIGFOOT® is a registered trademark of BIGFOOT 4x4, Inc., 6311 N. Lindbergh Blvd.,
Hazelwood, MO 63042, USA ©2004 All rights reserved.

Please note that every effort has been made to check the accuracy of the information
contained in this book, and to credit the copyright holders correctly. Picthall and Gunzi
apologize for any unintentional errors or omissions, and would be happy to include
revisions to content and/or acknowledgements in subsequent editions of this book.

ISBN: 978-1-4380-0918-6
Library of Congress Control No.: 2016933269

Manufactured by: Dream Colour (Hong Kong) Printing Ltd., Foshan, China

Date of Manufacture: June 2016

Printed in China

9 8 7 6 5 4 3 2 1

CONTENTS

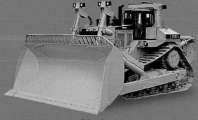

TRANSPORTERS

There is a different sort of truck for every job. Some big trucks are used for carrying cars, food, or animals from one place to another. These kinds of trucks are called transporters.

A long-distance articulated truck

Rigid trucks

This red truck is called a rigid truck because it cannot bend. Its driver has to be very good at driving around corners.

Can you point to?

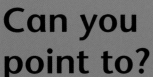
a wheel

a mirror

some lights

a grill

Bendy trucks

Trucks that can bend are called articulated trucks. A bendy truck is quite easy to drive around corners. This articulated transporter is carrying some cars and pick-up trucks.

A car transporter

What colors are these transporters?

LOGGERS

Trucks that carry logs are called loggers. A logger is big, tough, and powerful. It has to pull hundreds of logs in its trailer over rough, muddy tracks.

Hold tight

There are strong posts along each side of the trailer to keep all the logs in place.

Strong steel post

Why is this logger so big?

Harvester

This truck's long arm has a tool on the end called a harvester. It holds the tree while a sharp saw cuts through the wood.

Loader

This little loader picks up the logs and lifts them onto the trailer.

MIGHTY TRUCKS

In some countries there are massive trucks that can pull two, three, or even four trailers. These mighty trucks are called road trains. Road trains often carry their loads for thousands of miles!

Can you point to?

a circle

a diamond

a rectangle

some triangles

Twin trailers

This mega truck has two trailers joined together. It is called a B-double outfit.

Can you count the wheels on the road train?

Carrying fuel

This long road train is transporting huge fuel tanks on three trailers.

DIGGERS

Trucks called diggers are specially made for digging. They have different kinds of buckets for digging up different things. Some buckets are strong enough to cut through hard rock!

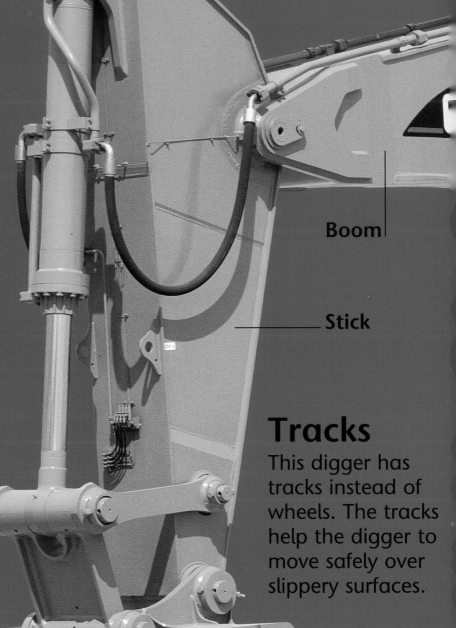

Boom

Stick

Loader arm

Tracks

This digger has tracks instead of wheels. The tracks help the digger to move safely over slippery surfaces.

Up and over

This digger has a loader arm that reaches over the top of the cab. A wire cage protects the driver as the digger tips its load out of the bucket.

Tracks

Bucket

Why are the tracks useful?

A strong arm

The driver controls the digger's arm from inside the cab. The arm picks up its load in the bucket and drops it in the right place.

Cab

BIG BULLDOZER

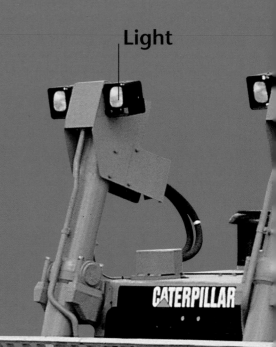

Light

Bulldozers are used for clearing the ground, ready for building. This enormous bulldozer can cut through almost anything. It pushes everything out of the way as it rumbles along.

Big bucket

This huge bucket has a sharp metal blade that can even cut through tree trunks.

Sharp blade

Exhaust

Cab

Can you point to?

a grill   a sprocket   a number

CARRYDOZER

D11R CD

What is this bulldozer used for?

Tracks

A good grip
The tracks on the bulldozer help it to grip, so it can climb up steep slopes too.

LOADERS

Trucks that load things into motortrucks are called loaders. They have a short, strong arm for lifting. A loader can carry lots of heavy rubble in its bucket.

Filling the tipper

The loader is emptying its big bucket of soil into the back of a red tipper motortruck. The loader can fill up the truck very quickly.

A huge load

This loader has forks instead of a bucket. It is carrying a heavy chunk of chalk. Diggers dig the chalk out of the ground.

Forks

Why does a loader have big tires?

Chunky tires

Loaders often have wide tires. Big tires help to keep the loader from falling over.

GIANT DUMPER

Enormous dumpers are used in quarries. They carry huge loads of rock from one part of the site to another. This mega dump truck is as big as a house!

Wow!

These children are three years old. See how tiny they are next to this mega truck!

What does a dumper do?

Can you point to?

a sign   air filters   a ladder

Super size

The cab is so high off the ground that the driver has to climb up a ladder to get inside.

Little by Little

This dumper is so gigantic that it cannot drive along ordinary roads. Other trucks have to take it to the site a little at a time.

CONCRETE MIXERS

Trucks called concrete mixers collect concrete in their drum and carry it to building sites. The big drum goes around and around all the time to mix the concrete and keep it flowing!

A small white concrete mixer

What pattern is on the big drum?

Extra wheels

This mixer has extra wheels on the back. The driver lowers these wheels when the mixer is traveling on public roads to the building site.

At the site

When a mixer arrives at the building site, the concrete is poured out of the back of the drum. It slides down a long chute, ready to use for building.

Chute

Drum

Extra wheel

Ladder

19

DUMP TRUCKS

Dump trucks are used for delivering sand, gravel, and other building materials to building sites. When dump trucks empty their loads, they tip up sideways or backwards.

An end dump truck

Side dump truck

This white dump truck has a body that can tip up sideways to deliver its load of wood chips.

What does a dump truck do?

Which of these is a side dump truck?

725

Can you point to?

a mud flap

a ram

a mirror

some lights

Tipping up

The front of this yellow end dump truck lifts up so that its load of earth can slide off the back.

21

ROAD BUILDERS

Building a new road takes a long time. There are lots of things to do before the tarmac goes on top. All these machines have their own special jobs.

Scraper

This truck is a scraper. It scrapes the top layer of soil off the ground so that the road can be put on top.

Roller

This big roller is very heavy. It rolls along the road to make it flat.

Grader

This machine is called a grader. It helps to make the ground all smooth before the road is built.

What job does a grader do?

Which machine makes the road flat?

GARBAGE TRUCKS

Garbage trucks help to keep all the streets clean and tidy. They collect everyone's garbage then take it away to be recycled or crushed.

A back-loader

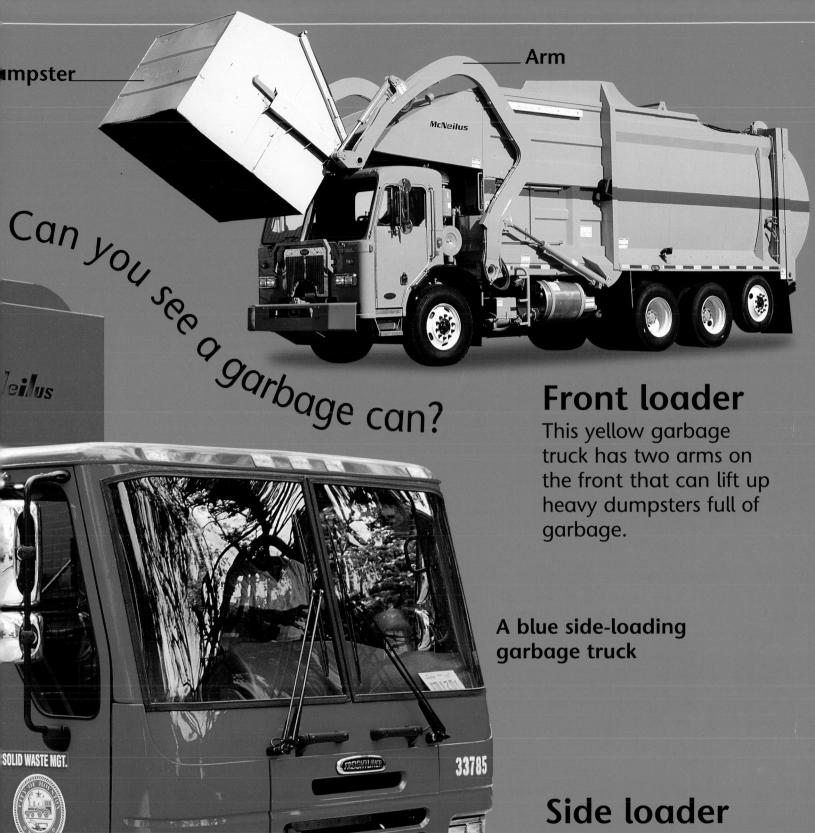

Dumpster

Arm

McNeilus

Can you see a garbage can?

Neilus

SOLID WASTE MGT.

FREIGHTLINER

33785

33785

Front loader

This yellow garbage truck has two arms on the front that can lift up heavy dumpsters full of garbage.

A blue side-loading garbage truck

Side loader

This blue garbage truck has an arm on the side for picking up big garbage cans. The arm grabs the garbage can, lifts it up and empties the garbage into the truck.

MEGA CRANES

Powerful cranes like this one are called mobile cranes. They have special steering and can travel on roads and over rough ground. Mobile cranes are used on all kinds of building sites.

Super strong

This giant crane can lift heavy loads high off the ground and move them safely to another place.

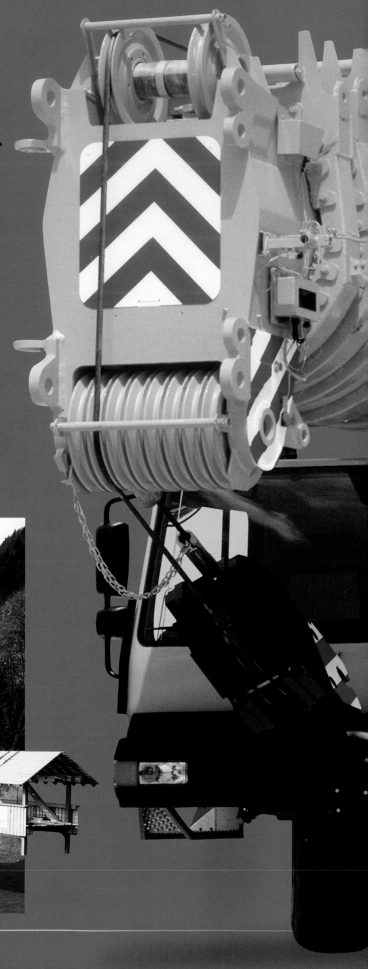

What are cranes used for?

On the move

Jib

The jib of this mobile crane folds down and lies on top of the cab when the crane is traveling along the road.

LIEBHERR

LIEBHERR

Can you point to?

an exhaust

a light

some chevrons

a pulley

TOUGH TRUCKS

Army trucks are strong and powerful. They have to be able to drive over rocks, mud, and sand, as well as on ordinary roads. Some army trucks can also drive through deep water!

An army truck traveling across a river

Can you see a clean spare tire?

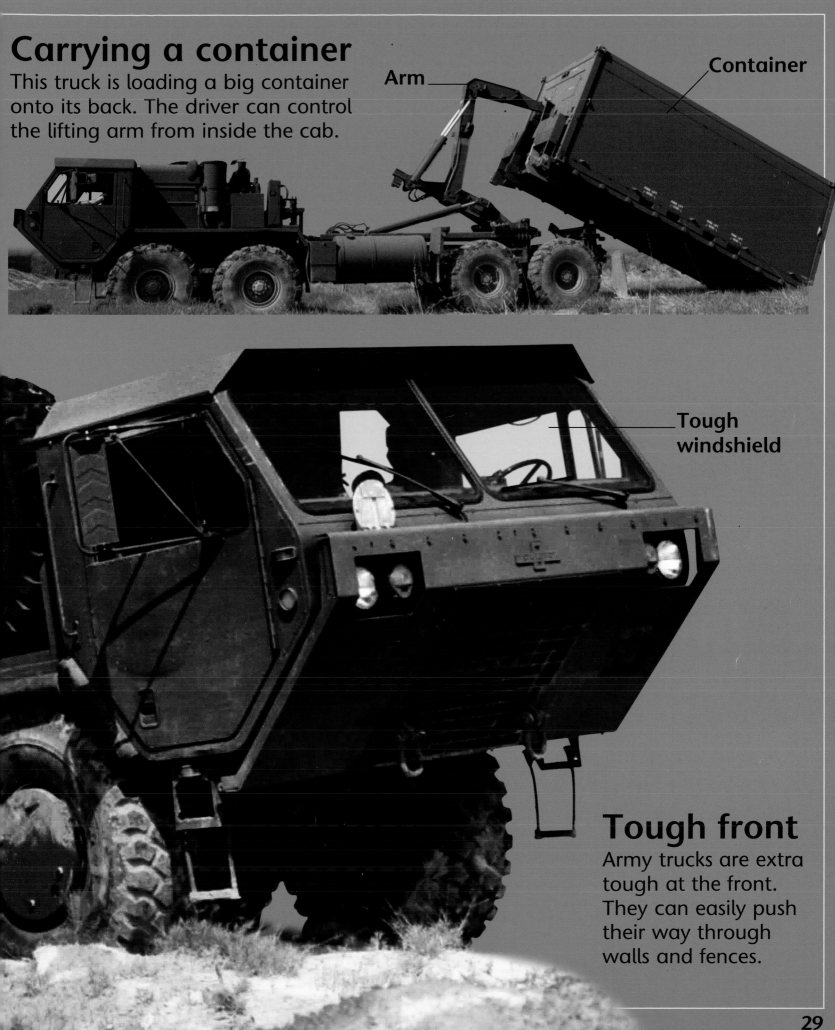

Carrying a container

This truck is loading a big container onto its back. The driver can control the lifting arm from inside the cab.

Arm

Container

Tough windshield

Tough front

Army trucks are extra tough at the front. They can easily push their way through walls and fences.

MONSTER TRUCKS

These huge pick-up trucks are specially made for racing and jumping. People enjoy watching them do tricks at shows. Monster trucks are so wide that they are not allowed on ordinary roads.

A monster truck called Blue Thunder

A Bigfoot truck

Biggest truck

This monster truck is called Bigfoot 5. It is the tallest, widest, heaviest pick-up truck in the whole world.

Wow!

These children are three years old. See how tiny they are next to this truck!

Jumping truck

Monster trucks are used to jump over old cars, just for fun. They are so tough that they crush the cars when they land on them.

Why do people drive jumping trucks?

LET'S MATCH!

Can you find all the matching pairs on this page?
Which truck do you like best?

LOADERS

DUMPERS

DIGGERS

LOADERS

DUMPERS

DIGGERS